YOUR KNOWLEDGE HAS VALUE

- We will publish your bachelor's and master's thesis, essays and papers

- Your own eBook and book - sold worldwide in all relevant shops

- Earn money with each sale

Upload your text at www.GRIN.com
and publish for free

Tanja Wittrien

Henry Fielding's technique of satire in "Jonathan Wild"

Analyzed with the help of Book IV, Chapter XIII and the function of the Heartfree subplot

GRIN Publishing

Bibliographic information published by the German National Library:

The German National Library lists this publication in the National Bibliography; detailed bibliographic data are available on the Internet at http://dnb.dnb.de .

Imprint:

Copyright © 2009 GRIN Verlag, Open Publishing GmbH
Print and binding: Books on Demand GmbH, Norderstedt Germany
ISBN: 978-3-656-46029-9

This book at GRIN:

http://www.grin.com/en/e-book/229828/henry-fielding-s-technique-of-satire-in-jonathan-wild

GRIN - Your knowledge has value

Since its foundation in 1998, GRIN has specialized in publishing academic texts by students, college teachers and other academics as e-book and printed book. The website www.grin.com is an ideal platform for presenting term papers, final papers, scientific essays, dissertations and specialist books.

1.) Analyse Fielding's technique of satire with the help of Book IV, Chapter XIII

If you take a closer look at Henry Fielding's *Jonathan Wild,* you quickly realise that the tone of the whole novel is highly satirical. Wild is described as an honorable man who achieved his remarkable 'greatness' by committing crimes and simply being a 'great prig'. The narrator goes even further and underlines this clear reversal of values by calling good people like the Heartfrees weak and detestable. Even though it seems like a praise at first, the term 'greatness' is in fact used to ridicule Wild's life.

But it's not only the exaggerated repetition of this word that shows Fielding's intention. His technique of satire can be exemplified by a close interpretation of Book IV, Chapter XIII.

Here we learn that Wild is still sitting in Newgate and that his „Cajoling the *Prigs*" and the „Exactions on the Debtors" (p.164) have led to an even worse corruption of the inmates. It's all about stealing and picking the Neighbour's pockets while virtue and goodness have become character traits which are at the utmost laughable. But this situation is not described as something bad or as an uncontrollable chaos. The narrator in this context uses the word „Glory" (p.164) where we would expect something entirely different. This underlines the whole satire of Fielding's novel. Things are turned around and the reader doesn't get what he expects because Jonathan Wild is called an honorable hero while he *really* is the prototype of the villain without a conscience. But this satirical style doesn't praise the lifestyle of Wild or any other criminal, it rather mocks it because even though the narrator talks about their 'Greatness', in the end they all die and none of them will be remembered as even remotely great.

Wild's preparations for his following trial are compared to those of the philosopher Socrates, only better. This clearly shows the enormous exaggeration which is thoroughly used in the whole book. Comparing Wild to one of the most important philosophers of all time and showing him as the winner of such a comparisons seems simply ridiculous. This is emphasised by the fact that all of Wild's great preparations fail and he is eventually sentenced to death. That this death is later on called honorable seems like a weak excuse for someone who doesn't want to admit his defeat and has therefore almost a comical effect. The whole complicated and long structure of this sentence and the way it is formulated only to end with the simple fact that Wild's efforts were useless add to this effect. Calling the way Wild has to die straight forward just „*to be hanged by the neck*"(p.165) afterwards shows clearly the intention behind the text.

Even though the reader in the beginning thinks that everything is meant exactly in the way it is written, hints like these quickly show Fielding's satirical approach and his artistic way of saying one thing while meaning the other.

The first quote in Book IV and the comparison to Alexander the Great continue the exaggeration and take it to another level. It seems delusional to call Wild's achievements something that will last forever because they didn't really have any impact on the world. He won't be remembered like Alexander the Great because he didn't conquer the Persian Empire or try to find the end of the world. He was just a criminal. The fact that people still know the name Jonathan Wild today is mostly due to Fielding and other writers who formed him as a fictional character. So even though Wild really existed, he can't nearly be compared to any important historical figure.

Another satirical technique can be found in the „sufficient Quantity of Mischief" (p.165) a 'hero' has to provide in his life to never be forgotten. The enumeration of „the Widow, the Orphan, the Poor, and the Oppressed" (p.165) by whom they have to be heartily cursed seems like a list you just have to tick off and not like a lifetime's achievement.

By using the second quote in this context, Fielding mocks Colley Cibber who tried to improve Shakespeare's *King John* and creates a connection between his and Wild's failure while still disguising it as a praise.

In the end Jonathan Wild is alone and the only comfort he can find lies in a bottle of alcohol. He doesn't have anyone left who cares for him and even when his wife visits all they do is fight.

In the centre of Fielding's novel stands the word 'greatness' that is intentionally used in a satirical way to describe Wild because he stands so clearly for everything this term doesn't signify. When used in a proper way greatness stands for all the good character traits and virtues a person can possess. It furthermore stands for the good deeds people do and their honorable reasons for doing them without expecting anything in return. In Wild's world everything comes with a price and nothing he does happens without some hidden agenda. His sole concern is making profit and his own well-being and this is the exact opposite of greatness.

In the end, almost nothing in this novel can be understood in the way it is actually said but as the exact opposite. Fielding creates an anti-world where everything is turned around and gives the whole story of Jonathan Wild an ironic and enormously satirical twist.

2. What is the function of the Heartfree subplot?

If you simplify the character images presented in Henry Fielding's *Jonathan Wild,* you'll come to the conclusion that there are two kinds of people standing in direct contrast to each other. These are on the one hand Jonathan Wild himself and on the other hand the Heartfree family.

While Wild represents the 'great' man who accomplishes so much by using his ingenious schemes, the Heartfrees are shown as stupid and boring people because they are loving and for them happiness is worth so much more than money. They are shown as the bad people and this is what makes the satire work so perfectly. The Heartfrees are the exact mirror image to Jonathan Wild because they stand for everything he doesn't have or doesn't want to have.

The subplot of Mrs. Heartfree's adventures stresses this idea because she gives an account for everything she went through just to get back to her husband and her children. Their emotional bond is just too strong to be broken by anything in the world and nothing could keep her from returning home. She is presented as the perfect lady who no other man can have, even though everyone desires her. But while her story starts off rather believable, the more she tells the more unrealistic it gets. Fielding again uses the technique of exaggeration to make his point because the things that happen to Mrs. Heartfree seem so absurd that you get the feeling she had to have been protected by some divine power to survive all this. And this could only be the case if she was the most perfect and best person in the world.

So even though the narrator talks of her and her husband as if he loathes them like Wild does, the true meaning behind all this lies in the satire of the whole novel. The exaggeration even goes so far that Mrs. Heartfree tells stories about giant monsters or mythical creatures like the phoenix and describes that they ate them (cf. p.152). This again makes a comical point because it takes this woman's naivety to the next level. She doesn't seem to have any idea how powerful and special a phoenix is and even though she knows it raises from its own ashes, she rather wants to eat it than watch it's extraordinary transformation. This is so ridiculous that it makes the whole situation rather funny and adds to the fact that Mrs. Heartfree doesn't care for any other treasure than her family. Wild on the other hand cares only for money and doesn't see any reason for trusting other people.

Where the Heartfrees rely on love, Wild relies on himself and while this is superficially described as the better way in the novel, its satire tells us that it's in fact the other way around. You can also find proof for that in the fairy tale ending the Heartfrees get in the end while Wild is simply hanged by the neck like an ordinary criminal. After everything the family went through, they don't have any trouble with money anymore, the eldest daughter marries Friendly and they're so exaggeratedly happy that their neighbours even call them „*the family of Love*" (p.181).

Another aspect that is shown by Mrs. Heartfree's story is the development of her character from extremely naive to more experienced and knowing. Due to the men she meets and the fact that they eventually all want something from her, she learns that she can't trust everyone. Even though it takes her some time to understand this, in the end it makes her a stronger woman and enables her to find her way home. This again adds to the concept of the mirror image the Heartfrees represent to Jonathan Wild because *his* character doesn't develop. He doesn't improve and his life doesn't change for the better. He just stays the way he is. While Mrs Heartfree learns from her mistakes, Wild doesn't learn anything. The moment we think he has a conscience and feels bad for what he has done to Mr Heartfree, he puts these thoughts aside and convinces himself that he doesn't care about it. His character stagnates and we learn another negative thing about Jonathan Wild because usually no good character in a novel just stays the same. You always have some kind of process they go through or progress they make but Wild doesn't do anything like that.

In the end, the Heartfrees help defining Wild and his character by serving as his mirror image because no matter what they do or what they are, he will always do and be the opposite of that.